FINANCE

Cloud Computing, Cyber Security, and Cyber Heist

BEGINNERS GUIDE TO HELP PROTECT AGAINST ONLINE THEFT IN THE CYBER WORLD

ALEX NKENCHOR UWAJEH

Finance: Cloud Computing, **Cyber Security** and Cyber Heist - Beginners Guide to Help Protect Against Online Theft in the Cyber World

CONTENTS

Introduction

There are a significant number of benefits to considering using cloud computing for your business needs. Yet, despite the numerous advantages, many business owners focus on the number of well-publicized  security breaches and hacking attempts made on big businesses that made the switch to the cloud.

For example, large companies such as Sony Pictures, Home Depot, Target, Hilton Hotels, Ashley Madison, and Anthem had their cloud computing systems hacked in the past year or so.

When such huge corporations get hacked with relative ease, it's enough to make anyone worry about the security of cloud computing and start wondering if their sensitive business information is somehow more vulnerable.

What you may not realize is that those big companies were perhaps using cloud storage improperly.

In truth, your business's important data is only ever as vulnerable as your security protocols.

The level of security on cloud-based systems is determined by two factors. The first is the amount of planning and technology used in engineering the business's security solution. The second is the business's ability to operate their computing systems securely without compromising information.

You have a huge level of control over the level of security safeguarding your sensitive business data. The key is learning ways to improve your business's operating protocols and ensure your data is always as secure as possible.

Cloud Computing, Hackers, and Data Security

One of the primary reasons so many hackers aim squarely at larger corporations using cloud-based computing systems is because that's where the money is. When you think about it, hackers have a job to do, just like everyone else. They have a limited amount of time in which to complete their job, so it makes sense to invest their time and efforts into businesses that are likely to give them the best possible results.

For this reason, hackers see large businesses using improperly secured cloud-based computing systems as being somewhat of a jackpot.

When you take all this into consideration, it suddenly appears as though the number of cyber-attacks against cloud-based systems has increased.

What many of those media reports fail to mention is that the sheer number of companies that have switched to a cloud environment has also increased. With more companies moving to the cloud and away from in-house data storage solutions and servers, of course it seems as though just those with cloud-based services are being targeted.

Most of those organizations are shifting their services and data into the cloud to take advantage of the increased flexibility, potential cost-savings, and the ability to scale services when they're required.

Unfortunately, far too many businesses rely on 'standard' cloud installation processes, instead of customizing their cloud computing solutions and security settings to their own individual needs. A standard installation can be replicated across lots of different enterprises and companies, which mean all the security settings are similar – and therefore become more vulnerable to cyber-attack.

Think about it this way: a thief could break into your home and steal your personal belongings. However, that same thief could also take a bigger risk by breaking into a bank and get a much bigger payoff. The bank has significantly more security in place than your personal home, but the bigger payoff is worth the risk to some thieves.

Now translate that same analogy into cloud computing. Hackers aim at larger cloud servers because that's where the bigger payoff is for them. Imagine a hacker breaking into a massive cloud database such as Gmail and grabbing data from millions of email accounts.

However, there will always be some hackers who aim at the easy targets, which include those companies with poorly secured in-house servers and data systems. The payoff might be smaller, but the work is much easier for them to get in and get back out again with your sensitive data.

When you boil it down, a cloud-based system is inherently more secure overall, as a larger cloud service provider such as Google or Amazon or Microsoft needs to focus strongly on being as secure as possible to reduce the threat of cyber-attack on millions of accounts.

In reality, hackers still target onsite data servers at the same frequency as they always did. It's merely the number of businesses that have moved to cloud services that has increased, which shows up on statistics as a sharp increase in cloud-based cyber-attacks.

Cyber-Crime Activities in the Cloud

The key factor in keeping cloud-based applications secure and reduce the risk of cyber-attack is to understand that security in the cloud should be a shared responsibility. The cloud provider needs to focus on ensuring that security strategies are as stringent as possible.

However, it's equally up to you as the customer to ensure that you understand what security measures you need to worry about to secure your data.

Some examples of the type of cyber-crime activities that cloud service providers face on a daily basis include:

Authentication Issues

Unauthorized access to systems can occur when someone username and password combination has been gained without the person's authorization.

Passwords can be obtained by people responding to phishing emails, or fake emails claiming to be from legitimate service providers asking the user to log into a false account.

Passwords can also be gained using key-logging software or hacked using brute force.

One of the easiest ways hackers gain access to cloud-based servers is by guessing people's password. A simple password using a pet's name or child's name is always easy for a hacker to work out, especially if those names are publicly available on social media accounts.

Likewise, choosing easy answers to secret questions where the answers are publicly available just makes a hacker's job easier.

Denial of Service Attacks

A Denial of Service (DoS) attack against a cloud service provider can leave users with no access to their accounts. DoS attacks occur by the attacker sending a flood of traffic to a website or group or websites on a host's server designed to overwhelm the servers and make them inaccessible.

Attacks can be launched using a 'botnet', which is a network of machines that distribute the source of the attack and make it more difficult to track its origins. A distributed denial of service attack is known as a DDoS.

Cloud Computing for Criminal Activities

Some cyber-criminals will use cloud-computing accounts to create new accounts used specifically for criminal purposes. Such accounts can be controlled using a botnet, which is then used to command and control a DDoS attack, or to launch a cyber-attack to overcome password restrictions on the cloud service provider's servers.

It's possible for criminals to create new cloud computing accounts using stolen credentials and stolen credit card details, which makes it even more difficult to track the origin of the attack.

Malware

While a cloud service provider's servers may be heavily monitored and updated with anti-virus and malware scanning capabilities, it is still possible for their servers to become vulnerable to infection.

For example, if one user's website is compromised with malware it's possible for the cloud provider's servers to become infected too, spreading to the virtual machines of multiple other clients.

Network or Packet Sniffing

Network or packet sniffing is all about the hacker intercepting network traffic. Any data that is transmitted across a network, including passwords, can be captured and read if they're not properly encrypted. In a cloud-computing environment, it's especially important to encrypt passwords and authentication codes properly, as they play an integral role in how the user accesses the cloud provider's services.

Access Management Issues

It's unfortunately common for many businesses to fail to restrict employee's access to cloud computing services once they leave their job. Once that employee leaves the organization, any passwords or other access information they have can allow them to compromise the business's data.

Former employees have been known to steal information, copy it, delete it, or otherwise alter it. For some, the intention behind the attack may be purely malicious, but for others it may be for the purpose of creating a competing business.

Physical Attacks on Servers

The servers provided by cloud service providers still need a physical home. Enormous data centers with intricate security systems in place usually house endless rows of physical servers that store every user's data.

While it's not common, it is possible for those servers and the data center to be physically attacked. In 2011, two people attacked a data center in Chicago, taking an employee hostage before using that employee's security pass and fingerprints to gain access to the center.

When you consider the sheer number of threats faced by cloud-based computing services, it's no wonder they're so vigilant about their security measures. They provide as much security surrounding protection of user data as possible, which makes them a significantly safer environment than an in-house data storage network system.

What they can't control is how their users treat their own personal security. That's up to you.

The Dark Web

The Dark Web is the shady underworld of the Internet. It's the place where hackers, cyber-criminals, and identity thieves thrive, and it bears very little resemblance to the Internet landscape you thought you knew. There's also a separate online realm, known as the Deep Web.

Before you can get some idea about the size and extent of the Dark Web and Deep Web, it might be important to draw an analogy.

Surface Web

Imagine the size and scope of the Internet, as you know it. All the search engines and social media sites and business websites and game sites you can access on a regular basis. Even some of those shady sites and online gambling sites sit on this level, especially if you found them on a random Google search.

These sites all form the Internet, as the majority of people understand it.

It's estimated that the public face of the Internet encompasses around **4%** of all the www content you see.

Deep Web

Now, imagine all those things are just the little tip of the iceberg showing above the surface. What lurks just below the surface is known as the Deep Web, or sometimes also called the Dark Net, and it's approximately **500 times** the size of the surface web.

Before you start thinking everything down in the Deep Web is illegal, immoral, sinister, or otherwise sleazy, consider some of the completely legal things hidden in obscurity down here:

1st Layer of the Deep Web

The first layer of the Deep Web is littered with web services and databases that conventional search engines can't index, such as Government databases and archived inner pages of private websites. These are completely legal. They're just inaccessible to the general public. Think of sites like members-only websites or password-protected content.

Even your Facebook newsfeed is down here on the first layer of the Deep Web, simply because it can't be indexed by the search engines.

Incidentally, this first layer is where most of your encrypted and unindexed data sits in the cloud.

2nd Layer of the Deep Web: The Dark Web

Sink a little deeper into the depths and you'll find the next layer of the Deep Web, known as the

Dark Web. This is the dark side of the Internet people think of when they picture shady underworld dealings and illegal activities.

The Dark Net is where most of the illegal, notorious, criminal, and downright sleazy side of the underworld thrives.

The Dark Net is the realm where those torrent-sharing sites, pirated software, pirated movie sites, and illegal download sites exist. It's where those highly illegal sites hide. It's where the database for the Hidden WikiLeaks hides.

There are also sections that focus on illegal gambling, selling guns, trafficking drugs, and offers of contract murder, among plenty of other things. Hackers and cyber-thieves also thrive down here.

It's also the domain of the Silk Road. We'll go into Silk Road and the Dark Web in some more detail a bit later in this chapter.

3rd Layer of the Deep Web

The third layer of the Deep Web is where the vast majority of deep traffic flows, and most of it is completely legal. It's also the layer that cyber-thieves find the most interesting.

This is where the corporate and government traffic lives on alternate, internal, and private networks, like LANs, WANs, and PANs. For example, your online bank account page is down here. The page where you type in your credit card information to complete an online purchase is down here.

It's hidden from the public level of the Internet because of its sensitive nature, which means it's delegated to limited-access only down in the Deep Web. And it's all totally legal.

Of course, some of the sensitive and private data stored in the cloud is also hidden down here in the 3rd layer of the Deep Web.

Unfortunately, this is the area hackers and cyber-thieves want to access to find their jackpots of sensitive data and private information. It's here where you need to be most vigilant about your organization's cyber-security.

The Silk Road

The Silk Road was an enormous black marketplace hidden in the depths of the Dark Web. It was best known as a platform for selling illegal drugs until the FBI seized it in October 2013. It didn't take long for The Silk Road 2.0 to emerge in its place and continue the thriving underworld business. Of course, that was also seized during a bust by the feds in November 2014.

The Diabolus Market was hastily renamed to Silk Road 3 Reloaded. Now The Silk Road 3.0 is up and active with support from multiple different cryptocurrencies, along with a range of other Dark Net underworld drug markets, including Green Road, Onion Pharma, Agora, and TheRealDeal.

Other dark marketplaces are designed to sell illegal drugs, weapons, guns, ammunition, hitmen for hire, assassinations, and a range of other sinister and illicit services.

Hackers thrive on the Silk Road, among other places on the Dark Web, as they're able to sell their hacking services to whoever wants them. For example, a listing found on Tor's Hidden Links directory for hidden Dark Web services has the following listing for a hacker's services for sale:

Rent-A-Hacker – Hacking, DDoS, Social Engineering, Espionage, Ruining People

Hackers and cyber-thieves are able to sell stolen information on the Dark Web, such as stolen identities, stolen Social Security numbers, fake IDs and driver's licenses, and stolen credit card information.

Cyber-thieves also use the Silk Road to sell skimmed credit card information, or to create brand new identities for people. There are multiple sites listed on Tor's Hidden Links directory for providing other forms of identification.

Tor's Hidden Links directory also lists a huge number of financial services available, including money laundering, high quality counterfeit money for sale, skimmed and stolen credit cards, and stolen login details for live bank accounts with actual US dollar balances in them.

Dark Web

The illegal side of the Deep Web is that area that is only accessible via the heavily encrypted network through a specialized routing protocol. This area is known as the Dark Web.

The Dark Web is the access via the encrypted network that is only accessible using a routing protocol such as The Onion Router, or TOR network.

The Onion Router (Tor) is an anonymous browsing client that uses the Tor Hidden Service Protocol to access sites on the Deep Web and the Dark Web.

The Tor network was created by the US Naval Research Laboratory for the purposes of creating a secure avenue for government communications. Since that time the network has entered the public domain.

The Tor browser can be downloaded for free and it's completely legal, as it's designed to keep the user's personal information secret. It's actually a nifty way to protect Internet users from identity theft. Some people use it to keep their kids safe on the Internet. Even law enforcement agencies use the Tor network for their anonymous tip lines and whistleblowing sites.

Users lurking in the underworld of the Dark Web don't access their version of the Internet straight through their computer. Rather, some will access the net using their Tor browser. Some will also use proxy servers, or a deeply layered structure of servers to route their traffic before it even reaches the anonymous Tor network. They also take particular care with their personal computer security settings to minimize the potential risks. If you're not careful when playing around in this realm, you can expect a visit from the FBI in due course.

The Dark Web has a number of hidden and anonymous email services and messaging services that allow people to communicate without revealing anything about their location or identity. There are anonymous forums and chatboards and several social networks, including the real Facebook's alternative .onion domain. Of course, regulars on the Dark Web tend to prefer BlackBook as their Dark Web social network of choice.

Website links on the Dark Web don't look much like the regular www hyperlinks the vast majority of people use on the Surface Web every day. Instead, links down in the Dark Web look more like this:

http://hos8et4ng6iar5zo7c.onion/

The sites on the Dark Web aren't indexed anywhere, so it's up to the individual site owners to list their .onion domains on a directory site such as Tor's Hidden Links.

The Tor Hidden Links directory displays the number of sites hiding on the Dark Web at around 30,000, which is about 0.03% of the total data and information online. Of course, that's just the number of sites that are voluntarily added to the directory.

By comparison, the public face of the Internet encompasses around 4% of the WWW content online and there are now more than a billion indexed websites.

There are also a massive number of unknown or unindexed sites lurking in the shadows that are only available to those who have access to the private link directly. Not everyone with a site on the Dark Web wants their link shared, displayed or made available. After all, many people are there to maintain their anonymity.

The remaining amount of information hiding on the Deep Web is simply private information that isn't indexed on search engines from government organizations, corporate networks, banks, and other private sites.

Bitcoins: Dark Web Currency

 Anyone who is unfamiliar with the Dark Web may wonder why transactions aren't traced or tracked through bank accounts and deposits by Interpol or various other cyber-crime law enforcement departments.

That's because the vast majority of transactions on the Dark Web marketplaces are conducted using Bitcoins, which is a digital cryptocurrency that gives the user a certain amount of anonymity. Bitcoin is a decentralized and unregulated type of currency that is free of the reins of any one government agency. As it's not backed by any government, the value of Bitcoin can fluctuate from day to day.

The user purchases Bitcoins, which are a completely legal currency and legitimate digital currency, and places them into their Bitcoin wallet. The buyer then transfers their Bitcoins into an anonymous wallet, where all of the Bitcoins are mixed with other Bitcoins that have been deposited by other users, so the flow of Bitcoins becomes untraceable.

Some marketplaces and commerce sites on the Dark Web use an escrow system to complete transactions. The buyer purchases items from the seller and pays for that transaction using the mixed Bitcoins in the anonymous wallet.

Sellers can exchange the Bitcoins they received for selling their products or services for real cash. Of course, there are multiple money laundering (and Bitcoin laundering) services available on the Dark Web, along with the ease of mixing Bitcoins in an anonymous wallet before withdrawing them anywhere, so there's very little trace of where they came from and who they're going to.

Global Cyber-Theft and Computer Forensics

International cybercrime and global cyber-theft are a major challenge for law enforcement agencies, as the laws in many countries aren't geared up to deal with online crime. In fact, it's common for many criminals to conduct their crimes over the Internet as a way to take advantage of the less severe punishments.

As a result, computer forensics is used to find evidence on computers and other forms of digital storage media. Computer forensics is a branch of digital forensic science that is most commonly associated with the investigation of cybercrime. Evidence recovered during an authentic computer forensics audit may be used as reliable evidence in U.S. and European court proceedings.

Believe it or not, one of the oldest methods for catching cyber-criminals is still the most effective for catching cyber-criminals. Undercover cybercrime law enforcement officers are responsible for a large number of busts and heists of Dark Web marketplaces in recent years.

Yet, the Dark Web and hackers aren't solely responsible for all of the global cybercrime problems. There is a broad range of cybercrimes that are investigated by computer forensics teams.

These include:

- **Hacking**: accessing a computer system illegally.

- **Cyber-Attacks**: denial of service (DoS) and distributed denial of service (DDoS) attacks designed to make a network unavailable to its intended users.

- **Phishing scams**: fraudsters send out emails that sometimes look like official communications from banks, asking customers to verify their log in details and passwords.

- **Data Espionage**: intercepting traffic and communications between users, including emails, chat conversations, or VoIP communications. This type of crime may also be called session hijacking or session riding.

■ **Identity Theft**: stealing private information, including login and password details, passport numbers, date of birth, Social Security numbers and other identifying details.

■ **Malware**: Malicious software, or malware, is designed to disrupt computer options, gather sensitive information, or to gain access to private computer systems. Access to a business's cloud computing account may be achieved if the device accessing the cloud service is compromised.

■ **Keyloggers**: Keystroke logging malware records the keys struck on a keyboard without the user being aware that their actions are being monitored. The intention is to capture the user's login and password details.

■ **Cyber-Forgery**: manipulating or falsifying digital documents.

- **Cyber-Fraud**: cyber-fraud offenses include credit card fraud, Internet banking fraud and online auction fraud.

- **Social Engineering**: a social engineering scam refers to a type of intrusion that fools the victim into downloading malware or giving out personal information. It's often used in emails or social networking chats and is effective for attacking well-protected computer systems.

- **Copyright Offenses**: distribution of illegally pirated software, movies, music, or books.

- **Trademark Violations**: cybersquatting is the act of using an Internet domain name with the intention of profiting from the use of a trademarked name belonging to someone else. The cybersquatter will then offer to sell the domain to the company that owns the trademark at an inflated price.

- **Cyber-terrorism**: spreading propaganda, gathering information, publishing training material, financing terrorist organizations, or preparing for real-world attacks.

■ **Cyber-Laundering**: conducting crimes through the use of virtual currencies or via cryptocurrencies. This section of cybercrime also includes people laundering cash by using online gaming, through digital cryptocurrencies, or using micro-payments.

With so many different cyber-crime activities to watch for, protecting your security and preventing an attack can seem daunting. Fortunately, there are some things everyone can do to reduce the risk of becoming the target of a cyber-attack.

Prevention for your organization

Knowing that there are hackers and cyber-thieves lurking on the Dark Web should give you some incentive to review your organization's security settings. However, did you know that a large percentage of security breaches and data leaks come from within the organization itself? Many employees may not even realize they could be compromising the company's computer

security with their actions, simply due to lack of training.

Many organizations may also be compromised by outdated anti-virus software and a lack of proper security implementation.

No matter whether your computing systems are on an in-house network server or hosted in the cloud, here are some things you can do to prevent a cyber-attack for your organization:

Check Current Cyber Health

It's important to check what the current health status of your computing systems looks like before you start updating or upgrading anything. Hire an IT security consultant to give you a complete overview of your cyber health needs to ensure nothing is overlooked and have a PEN (Penetration) Test performed on your network to see how well it might withstand a cyber-attack.

Implement Security Measures

Be sure your company's anti-virus software is up to date across all of your computer terminals and any tablet PCs or other mobile devices that connect to the organization's network. Back up all company data regularly and ensure backup copies are stored securely.

Secure internal network servers and connections, and verify the security settings of any cloud-based services you use.

Consider adding an extra layer of protection with Multifactor Authentication (MFA). This is a type of security system that requires more than one method of authentication to verify the user's identity that can be invaluable for protecting the identities of users at the same time as securing access to corporate networks.

Protect Against Malicious Attacks

Protect your organization from malicious traffic attacks with DDoS (Distributed Denial of Service) protection. There are three primary types of DDoS attacks that could cripple a server, network or corporate infrastructure. These are:

- **Volume-based attacks**: a swarm of requests, usually showing illegitimate IP addresses, intended to overwhelm site bandwidth with a flood of traffic.

■ **Protocol attacks**: sending open requests (TCP/IP requests) with fake IPs in an effort to drain resources so they're unable to answer legitimate requests, making the system unavailable for legitimate users.

■ **Application layer attacks**: also called Layer 7 attacks, these are slow and stealthy attacks that send seemingly harmless requests intended to bring down a web server.

You can fortify against malicious traffic attacks by ensuring that servers are patched promptly. Use a small backup circuit and segregate any key servers. Then test your anti-DoS service to be sure key employees or consultants know what to do in case of an attack.

There are many security solutions available that offer excellent DDoS protection services. Be sure your investment in any DDoS protection is in proportion with the actual business risk, but also ensure that your protection maintenance can be scaled as your business needs evolve.

Web App Attacks

If your organization uses online payment processing facilities or online point-of-sale (POS) software, it's important to protect against web app attacks and POS intrusions. Businesses in the retail, information, hospitality, and manufacturing industries are particularly at risk here.

You can help to prevent misuse of stolen information or exploitation of vulnerabilities by using two-factor authentication for transactions. Consider switching your current web apps to a static content-management system. Set your web apps to lock accounts after a specified number of failed login attempts, and ensure that you monitor any outbound connections.

To reduce the risk of POS intrusions, limit any remote access to your POS systems by third-party companies and enforce strong password policies. Ideally, POS systems should use two-factor authentication.

Create Cyber-Security Policies

Create some clearly-worded cyber-security policies and train all company employees on IT risk. Determine precisely what your expectations are in terms of cyber-security and document it. Include a 'safe-use' flash drive policy for all employees to reduce the risk of a compromised flash drive being used in your business systems.

Review all company user accounts and remove access to any former employees, if this hasn't been done already. Set up control systems to watch for data transfers out of the organization to protect against data theft from inside the company.

Train Employees on Cyber-Security Policies

Invest the time and effort to train every employee within the organization on your company's cyber-security policies. It's important that every person within your business understands the importance of acting responsibly with company assets and data.

All staff members also need to understand their roles and your expectations of any internet and intranet usage during working hours, including accessing personal emails and social media on company devices and connecting unsecured mobile devices to local Wi-Fi networks.

Prevention for the home user

While ensuring that all company and business IT systems are secured, it's also important to protect home computers and personal devices against cyber-attack.

Here are some simple steps you can take to reduce the risk of a cyber-attack on personal systems:

Home Computing Systems

- Keep all of your operating systems (OS), Antivirus, antispyware, and other software up-to-date

- Enable your firewall

- Secure your wireless network with WPA encryption and set a strong password

- Install any security updates or patches for your operating system promptly

- Make sure your home wireless network is secure

- Never download or install unfamiliar programs onto your system

- Don't insert untrusted thumb drives or data storage drives into your computer

Passwords

- Create secure passwords for any online accounts that contain a combination of upper- and lower-case letters, numbers and symbols

■Don't use publicly-available names or phrases in your password (such as pet's or kid's names)

■Don't use the same password for multiple services

■Change passwords regularly

■If necessary, use a password management service to keep track of different passwords for various services

■Don't use the option for your operating system to automatically remember your passwords

■Never give out your passwords to anyone

File Usage and Access

■Encrypt your files

■Disable file sharing on your computer

■Delete any cookies saved on your computer

■Delete your internet browsing history regularly

Online Activity

- Always log on directly to business website. Don't click through to the website from an email link

- Make sure a website is secure before you enter any personal information: i.e. make sure the web address starts with the prefix https://

- Think before you click: Be extra careful while downloading random free applications

- Never use public Wi-Fi for financial transactions. Only use trusted private computers or devices to keep your information secure.

- Set your Internet browser to block pop-up ads. Some unscrupulous people use pop-up ads to install malicious software on your computer.

- Be vigilant about phishing websites that look like legitimate business sites, but are really fake sites seeking your personal information.

Avoid any site asking for personal information that could compromise your online identity.

Email Usage

- Change your email settings so that attachments aren't automatically downloaded

- Never click on links in emails, even if you think the email appears legitimate. If you hover your mouse over the link in an email you can often see the website address under the visible link may be very different to the anchor-text written there for you to see.

- Type website addresses into your browser directly to ensure you are taken to the correct site, instead of a malicious site.

- Never open attachments in emails. Set your email settings so you don't' automatically download attachments.

- Never give out personal information in an email, such as passwords, credit card numbers or bank account details

Social Media

Be careful about how much information you give out on social media. It's surprising how much information people can gather about you without your knowledge just with simple social media updates.

- Your kid's names and pet's names are often publicly available just by chatting about them or posting pics of them.

- If you complain about the service at your bank on social media, a hacker now has that information about what company you do your banking with, making you an easy target for identity theft.

- If you post photos of your home or your car, blur out the house number or license plates, as these things also give away a lot about your identity to unscrupulous people.

- Don't answer silly questions on social media that ask you to enter your full name and date of birth to see a cool pic pop up when you're done.

Smartphone Security

Most people are aware of the importance of protecting their home computer systems, but they don't always consider doing the same thing with mobile devices.

The number of people accessing the Internet and using mobile apps is increasing daily. Of course, many smartphones are prone to viruses, malware, keyloggers and theft.

If your cell phone was stolen by an unscrupulous person, it's likely the thief would have access to your online banking details, complete with passwords and PINs, your emails, your social media accounts, passwords to your home Wi-Fi connection, and a range of other personal information.

You can protect your smartphone by doing the following:

■ Set a pin code or password on your lock screen. It provides an extra layer of difficulty for a thief trying to access your phone

- Install and enable remote services, such as setting a remote lock, remote wipe, and GPS location for tracking a lost or stolen phone

- Back up your data regularly by copying documents, pictures and other data to your computer.

- Use encryption where you can. Not every smartphone operating system offers this option, but if you can you should encrypt your data, including the external memory card, or SD card.

- Use smartphone antivirus software to reduce the risk of infection with malware or viruses

- Don't connect to untrusted Wi-Fi access points. Many public Wi-Fi points, such as airports, coffee shops, or fast-food restaurants may have compromised connectivity.

- Always enable operating system updates and app updates promptly to reduce the risk of being exposed to attack

Monitor Your Credit Report File Regularly

A big part of being vigilant about identity theft is making sure someone doesn't already have your information and is using it for their own gain – and to your detriment. The sooner you catch any suspicious activity, the easier it is to stop it.

Order a copy of your credit report file regularly and review it carefully for any transactions or entries that don't look familiar.

Protect Physical Documentation

Identity theft isn't limited to just your online activities. It's also important you protect your identity on any physically printed documentation.

Paper documents, such as bank statements, utility bills, tax returns, and driving license information should be filed securely. Always shred any documents you do not need, especially if they contain your personal information.

Protect Your Children Online

Anyone with kids who use the Internet faces a bit of a challenge. On the one hand, it's important for kids to experience new technologies. On the other hand, there are plenty of inherent dangers for kids online.

Fortunately, there is security software available that can help to restrict the amount of things kids are able to see and do online. Perhaps the biggest issue parents face is having their child preyed upon by a predator online. Using specific software can help to filter the types of sites kids are able to surf.

Despite the ability to restrict the type of content they can view, kids can also unknowingly compromise your family's privacy and identity.

It's important that children are taught how important it is to protect their personal information. Many child-oriented websites focus on obtaining information from kids by asking them to fill in surveys or forms in exchange for a prize.

What kids may not realize is that they give out a lot of personal information when registering for these things, including their gender, age, and favorite place to hang out.

Social media sites and chat rooms also pose numerous dangers to kids. Ensure your kids understand the basic rules for using any social networking sites, including protecting their passwords and being careful about posting identifying information.

Teach kids not to download games or apps from unfamiliar or untrusted sources. Some parents allow kids to download music, games and apps that may require credit card information, so ensure that they're monitored when making purchases. Never allow kids to enter your credit card details into an unsecured website.

Kids can explore, learn and enjoy their online interest safely, but there are some simple steps every parent can take to protect them from online threats and inappropriate content.

Conclusion

Protecting your family against cybercrime doesn't need to be a daunting task. In fact, as long as you remain vigilant about your personal information and take appropriate steps to protect yourself, you should never experience any major problems.

Of course, if you own a business or company, your livelihood could be severely affected if your organization becomes the target of a cyber-attack from someone with malicious intent. Implement strong cyber-security strategies and work closely with an IT security consultant to ensure your business computing systems are protected at all times.

As long as you stay on top of your security needs, you'll be taking positive steps to reduce the risk of ever becoming a target of cyber-attack or cyber-theft.

Other Available Books:

- In The Pursuit of Wisdom: The Principal Thing

- Investing in Gold and Silver Bullion - The Ultimate Safe Haven Investments

- Nigerian Stock Market Investment: 2 Books with Bonus Content

- The Dividend Millionaire: Investing for Income and Winning in the Stock Market

- Economic Crisis: Surviving Global Currency Collapse - Safeguard Your Financial Future with Silver and Gold

- Passionate about Stock Investing: The Quick Guide to Investing in the Stock Market

Guide to Investing in the Nigerian Stock Market

- Building Wealth with Dividend Stocks in the Nigerian Stock Market (Dividends - Stocks Secret Weapon)

- Bitcoin and Digital Currency for Beginners: The Basic Little Guide

- Child Millionaire: Stock Market Investing for Beginners - How to Build Wealth the Smart Way for Your Child

- Christian Living: 2 Books with Bonus Content

- Beginners Quick Guide to Passive Income: Learn Proven Ways to Earn Extra Income in the Cyber World

- Taming the Tongue: The Power of Spoken Words

- The Power of Positive Affirmations: Each Day a New Beginning

- The Real Estate Millionaire: Beginners Quick Start Guide to Investing In Properties and Learn How to Achieve Financial Freedom

- Business: How to Quickly Make Real Money - Effective Methods to Make More Money: Easy and Proven Business Strategies for Beginners to Earn Even More Money in Your Spare Time

- Money: Think Outside the Cube: 2-Book Money Making Boxed Set Bundle Strategies

If you would like to share this book with another person, please purchase an additional copy for each recipient. Thank you for your support and thanks for reading this book.

www.ingramcontent.com/pod-product-compliance
Lightning Source LLC
Chambersburg PA
CBHW051124050326
40690CB00006B/799